WALKING

on UNEVEN GROUND

Why Kids Outdoor Zone is a Critical Ministry for Today

TJ GREANEY & RICK MAGEE

KOZ PUBLISHING COMPANY
Austin, Texas

KOZ is a 501c3. You can support the mission of Kids Outdoor Zone with donations of land, cash, or vehicles. Just go to KidsOutdoorZone.com or call 512-292-1113 for more information.

CONTENTS

IF YOU CONTINUE THIS QUEST, YOU MAY JUST
ENTER THE SEAL TEAM FOR JESUS TRAINING.
YOU MAY FIND THE MISSION
YOUR HEART HAS LONGED FOR
AND IT WILL CHANGE YOU FOREVER.

INTRODUCTION

Every man needs a mission. The young men who choose to join the armed services or law enforcement are answering a calling to a mission. The guys who choose Navy Seal or Special Forces are especially tuned in. The (crazy) guys with the squirrel flying suits are longing to feel, hear, be a part of something bigger than themselves. They long for meaning and adventure. So do you. Rick Magee and I (TJ Greaney) found that mission in Kids Outdoor Zone (KOZ). We have also trained and seen men come alive after understanding the principles in this book and the effect that knowing them has on their heart.

Alas, too many men today have given up on the "call of the wild." For many they have never even experienced it. The incredible life-change and emotion that comes from a deeper understanding of who they are and how feeling the Holy Spirit in their hearts changes them. They settle for less than mediocrity. They choose to follow and cheer for a college football team or professional basketball team as their outlet for what it is they can't define in their hearts. They pour into working and make success or money their calling, only to be let down that the latest deal or latest bonus just didn't fill their cup.

Men in the church may be even worse. In a recent conference for pastors, I found myself looking into the eyes of men worn out from trying to get the men in their church to engage. "I can get them to church on Sunday. They do the once a quarter breakfast, but man, to get them to dig deep, do the stuff that will bring them alive is wearing me out," one Pastor said. He is experiencing the lethargic hearts of so many men today in the church. Just showing up, checking the box, then heading to the buffet lunch.

I was talking to my buddy David Murrow; he wrote the book *Why Men Hate Going to Church*. During our conversation he said, "Men's ministry is brutal. Trying to get them to do anything is hard. I'm switching my focus to other things in my writing now because it just doesn't seem to be making a lot of impact." At a recent meeting of The National Coalition of Men's Ministry, NCMM, I heard the same thing. Lots of ministry leaders trying but the men of the church are just not participating.

If you are reading this, you are in an elite group of men seeking their hearts. Really. So brother, consider yourself pinned. You have been given a badge of honor and if no one else tells you this, we are dang proud of you. Thank you. If you continue this quest, you may just enter the Seal Team for Jesus training. You may find the mission your heart has longed for and it will change you forever.

This short book should be a tool for you to use to open your heart and seek the voice of Jesus. Even if you do not choose to start a Kids Outdoor Zone group in your church, I would encourage you to listen to your heart right now. The things you learn here will give you input on some things going on in our world, our churches. There may be things that you are experiencing in your family or that you experienced personally. Allow yourself to hear, feel, stay in the moment. Does God want you to act on it?

After a recent presentation at a men's conference, I had a guy come up to me and share with me how he was convicted to step deeper into his relationship with his kids. He said the things he learned opened his eyes to just how much was happening to them and how much he was ignoring. "I go to work, coach their soccer team, but I don't really hear what is happening at school, in their hearts. I need to sit with them by a campfire and let God teach me to hear them." So good. We didn't care if he started a KOZ group; he is realizing he needs to be more. He is stepping into a rescue mission for his heart, his kids, his family. Go, Jesus, go!

When the Holy Spirit catches a man's heart, he will begin to come alive. When he feels in his heart the presence of Jesus, he begins to live differently. Religiosity kills men. They hear that if they perform, they are good Christians. If they tithe, set up chairs, and show up to meetings, they are maximizing their walk. That is not a walk. It is drudgery. Yes, we need to do all those things as a member of the church body. Absolutely. But those things are not what fills your heart with this unbelievable emotion to do better, grow, challenge yourself. A man who is moved by the Holy Spirit is constantly becoming a new man.

What does all this have to do with outdoor ministry for boys? It's because these men—the ones who commit to walking with the fatherless boys in their communities and church, the men who walk with their sons and the fatherless boys—these are the men who are stepping up, stepping in, world changers. These are the men you want to run with in your church. They see things differently. They are the men that when the going gets tough, when the posse needs to gather, you can count on them. These men have drawn their side arms. They will fight for good.

These are the men the boys need to train under. These are the ones who will transform the lies of the evil one who has tried to convince our boys that a father can't be trusted. Satan's lies today tell boys that men are not to be trusted. That women are objects. The KOZ men are the ones who will teach our boys to walk uneven ground and do hard things. These are the men we want our boys to learn from. These men will ride or die for the boys, the men of our next generation.

Step into this information with an open heart. Some of it may be shocking, maybe not. But after you read it, ask yourself one question. "So, now what? What is it I am going to do? What is it, Jesus, you want me to do? I can't not do anything anymore." Then listen.

God never said that the journey would be easy,
but He did say that the arrival
would be worthwhile.

MAX LUCADO

CHAPTER 1

THE FATHERLESS FACTOR

"Houston, we have a problem." These words have been echoed through the decades since that legendary flight of Apollo 13 in 1970. Astronaut Jack Swigert told mission control the crew faced the failure of an oxygen tank two days into the mission. Without enough oxygen to proceed would have meant certain death of the astronauts and the demise of the operation. They were forced to abort and return to earth after just orbiting the moon once.

Today as we look at the landscape of our communities, we see men withdrawing emotionally and physically, erupting in anger, fathering children indiscriminately, facing incarceration, enticed and led away by the fruit of the vine (alcohol). In unprecedented numbers, they are leaving the home and their wives and kids to the vulnerabilities of a hard world that has little mercy on the family. In the words of our astronaut friend—America, we've got a problem. Church, we have a problem. Moms and little girls around the country, we've got a problem. The problem is the absence of the biblically masculine male. The man, the father, that will provide, protect, and pastor his family is missing and at alarming rates in the American home and the homes all around the world.

The problem is real, and its effects can be seen in Danny who came to summer camp. Danny was assigned his cabin and bunk and introduced to his cabin leader. His mom told us that he had been super excited about camp and the adventure that was promised. Danny is a kid like many other nine-year-old boys, blonde hair with a few flowing locks, freckles, braces, a little on the skinny, lanky side. When he got to camp, he was very observant and cautious, but excited nonetheless. Danny began the first day questioning the authority of his cabin leader (Jr. KOZ leader, an older KOZ boy trained to lead at camp). He was smart and subtle; he would only do it when the older adult leaders were not around. By the second day, he was outright rejecting the cabin leader's direct requests and direction. But still, Danny kept it hidden and the cabin leader didn't want to be that guy that took every little thing to the adult KOZ leaders. By the third day, the cabin leader was at his wit's end from all the sarcasm, rejection, poor attitude, and smart mouth. He asked permission to take a walk, a long walk. That was when the adult KOZ leaders pressed in. Danny had been acting out for three straight days and the Jr. leader was worn out.

If someone was living in a cocoon of a protected healthy portion of society (albeit I'm not sure where that would be) they might ask, "Are you sure this is a problem?" Let's take a look at some statistics that shed light on this issue.

The statistics below have one thing in common, FATHERLESSNESS.

- 85 % of all children who exhibit behavioral disorders
- 90 % of all homeless and runaway children
- 71 % of all high school dropouts

- 75 % of all adolescent patients in chemical abuse centers
- 63 % of youth suicides
- 80 % of rapists motivated by displaced anger
- 70 % of juveniles in state-operated institutions
- 85 % of all youth sitting in prison

All come from a FATHERLESS home. This is staggering! When dad leaves, life can begin to fall apart for a boy. Stay in this struggle with me a few moments more.

A child from a fatherless home is also:

- 5 times more likely to commit suicide
- 32 times more likely to run away
- 20 times more likely to have behavioral disorders
- 14 times more likely to commit rape
- 9 times more likely to drop out of school
- 10 times more likely to abuse drugs
- 20 times more likely to end up in prison

The statistics above don't address what may be going on inside the average adult man either. The meter reader, pipefitter, HVAC technician, factory supervisor, vice president, general manager, pastor, or business owner who is surviving his own absent father wounds. These wounds cause men to be present in body but emotionally unavailable as dads, husbands, fathers, and friends. It is actually all too common as they attempt, many times unknowingly, to survive fatherlessness themselves.

"Fatherlessness, the ironic tragedy, is the unavailable dad who grew up with these wounds who often replicates the problem in his own children, thus growing the issue exponentially in society." Rick Magee

The adult KOZ camp leaders stepped into the situation with Danny. There were immediate consequences issued and apologies required. That evening, one by one, Danny apologized to the leaders. Danny told them that his mother and father had recently divorced, and his mom informed him on the way to camp that she was going on her first date since the divorce. Danny's world was turning upside down...again. Before that night was over, the young KOZ leaders surrounded Danny and prayed over him and told him that they were there for him. Danny saw the love of Christ through those young men and he surrendered his life to Christ.

For Danny, the KOZ men of this camp and the other KOZ boys are in his life now. The KOZ ministry will play an ongoing role in teaching him life skills, biblical virtue, and most of all, God's love. A boy needs a man to become a man.

On April 17, 1970, Apollo 13 and its crew returned safely to earth. The astronauts and Mission Control immediately made the adjustments necessary to get the men and their space craft home. The story would have ended very differently if the crew and Mission Control would have been casual or unconcerned about the loss of the critical oxygen tank. Disaster and failure would have ensued.

It is the same to be said of the issue of fatherless. It seems that much of America and the church today are not even willing to admit there is a problem. And many who do realize there is a problem are not willing to make the necessary adjustments to correct course. One by one, community by community, the boys are losing their way. I'm not smart enough to develop a timeline on when this is going to create unrecoverable disaster for our culture and country, but if left unaddressed, it most certainly will.

We need to realize and admit that we are faced with a crisis, a tragedy. Jesus, we have a problem.

Father of the fatherless
and protector of widows
is God in his holy habitation.
PSALM 68:5

I KNEW I NEEDED TO GET INVOLVED
WITH SOME MEN AT CHURCH
AND BECOME A PART OF MEN'S MINISTRY,
SO I PONIED UP.

· · ·

MY HEART WAS HUNGRY
FOR SOMETHING DEEPER,
SOMETHING REAL.

CHAPTER 2

THE MEN OF THE CHURCH

I remember back when I first really committed to a men's Bible study. It seemed the only ones I ever heard of were at 6:30am and I hated that. I have always been a morning person so it wasn't a problem with the time, but to go and get around other people that early was what I was not all that enthusiastic about. I like to start my day early but slow and quiet. However, I knew I needed to get involved with some men at church and become a part of men's ministry, so I ponied up.

Back when I first started going to the Bible study, I was a good soldier. I listened well, read what I was supposed to for years. Then one day as I sat in the hard plastic chair fashioned in rows early on Wednesday morning, I blurted out, "bull s##t." I went into a long dissertation on how it was fine and dandy that the guy teaching was telling us all what to do. He did that every week. On that day all his wonderful and eloquent scripture just seemed like another morning of empty words that I just could not fit into my daily life. I needed real life examples; I needed him to share his heart. I needed a guy to cry when he talked about his kids or his wife and how maybe, just maybe, he was not perfect.

I was tired of being talked to and not included in a conversation. I was tired of the bland, plastic, and rigid discourses. My heart was hungry for something deeper, something real. I had earned the right to hear what these men were really like. Did we have anything in common? Anything? This was the beginning of my heart joining me in my journey with Christ.

Men are a tough crowd when it comes to church. Getting them in the door, getting them to a Bible study, can be really difficult. Early mornings before work, pancake breakfasts (bacon), and speakers all seem to work some. For me, I needed it to be simple, to be real, and I would then learn to trust you. Talk over me, try to put me in a box with a bunch of guys I don't fit in with, I'm not coming.

Washington Area Coalition of Men's Ministries reports:

- 95 % of men say they don't have male friends; less than 1/3 of men in church say they have a friend.

- 90 million men are not involved in any kind of discipleship. Only 6 million men are involved in discipleship--only 1 out of every 18 men.

- On any given Sunday there are 13 million more adult women than men in America's churches.

- This Sunday almost 25 % of married, churchgoing women will worship without their husbands.

- Midweek activities often draw 70 to 80 % female participants.

- More than 90 % of American men believe in God, and 5 out of 6 call themselves Christians. But only

2 out of 6 attend church on a given Sunday.
The average man accepts the reality of Jesus Christ
but fails to see any value in going to church.

- Fewer than 10 % of U.S. churches are able
to establish or maintain a vibrant men's ministry.

- Fewer than 1 % of churchgoing men participate
in any sort of ongoing men's ministry program.

- As many as 70 % of men have actively sought out
pornography this year.

- As many Christians will divorce as
non-Christians.

For every 10 men in the church:

- 9 will have kids who leave the church
- 8 will not find their jobs satisfying
- 6 will pay the monthly minimum
on their credit cards
- 5 will have a major problem with pornography
- 4 will get divorced affecting 1,000,000
per year

Boys are the same. How many boys today want to be at
school all week being told to be good, sit still, pay attention, then turn around and do it again on Sunday morning? There is a direct correlation between why boys don't
want to go to church and why men don't go to church. If
it does not feel relevant to their lives, they are out. If it
does not feel real, they are not coming. What they believe
and have heard in a lot of cases is true. At church you get
told what to do, what not to do, and give us money.

What if the men and the boys got together, especially boys without dads, and hung out around a campfire? What if they all just picked one Saturday a month and hiked, shot bows, went fishing, talked? Real talking. What if the boys heard the men tell stories of how they made mistakes, how they made decisions to choose good over evil? What if the boys knew that no matter what, these men would love them, care for them, and not leave them like their dads did, their mom's boyfriend did, like every man in their life ever has?

What if the men finally found a ministry they could be a part of that was real, hands on, doing something they felt made a real difference? If they could actually see boys being rescued because of the ministry work they did. Men are desperate for a mission, a posse to ride with, a place they can truly see the fruit of their work. Yet so often the offer is setting up chairs, passing the basket, helping park cars, or babysitting in a classroom for forty minutes on Sunday.

That is where the ministry of Kids Outdoor Zone (KOZ) came from—exactly where. Men who needed something powerful to be a part of. They needed something where they could feel the effects of their works, the moving of the Holy Spirit. A ministry where they knew without a doubt Jesus was directing their steps. A place they could feel and see the rescue of their hearts and the boys in their community.

THE CALLING: Job 29:12, "For I was a savior to the poor when he was crying for help, to the child with no father, and to him who had no supporter."

THE MISSION: Proverbs 22:6, "Train up a boy in the way he should go, when he is old he will not depart from it."

THE REWARD: Matthew 25:21, "His master told him, 'Well done, good and trustworthy servant! Since you have been trustworthy with a small amount, I'll put you in charge of a large amount. Come and share in your master's joy!'"

The only use of an obstacle is to be overcome. All that an obstacle does with brave men is not to frighten them, but to challenge them.

WOODROW WILSON

HIS HEART LONGS TO EXPLORE THE WOODS AND BACKYARD,
THE MOUNTAINTOPS AND DITCHES.
GOD CREATED HIM IN THIS
BEAUTIFUL AND POWERFUL WAY.

CHAPTER 3

THE BOY

A boy was designed to skin his knee. Really. A boy wants to jump his bike off the ramp he built from broken boards and rusty nails. He wants to hang upside down in the tree until his face is purple. He wants to know about wild and dangerous things that crawl and slither, hop and growl. His heart longs to explore the woods and backyard, the mountaintops and ditches. God created him in this beautiful and powerful way.

Society today has embraced a false narrative about our boys. It's one that tells the boy he has to sit still, and if he does, he is good. They tell our boys that the desire to walk uneven ground is not safe and should be avoided. The feminization of boyhood is a real topic of societal conversation. They are seeking to transform our boys into something they are not created to be. You can't tell a chicken to be a dog, a cat to be a horse, or a boy to be something he is not. These things are killing our boys from the inside out and the damage will be long term. Generations.

Effects of Fatherlessness (or Motherlessness) – US Data: Behavioral Disorders/ Runaways/High School Dropouts/ Chemical Abusers/Suicides

- 85 % of all children who exhibit behavioral disorders come from fatherless homes

(Source: Center for Disease Control)

- 90 % of all homeless and runaway children are from fatherless homes *(Source: U.S. D.H.H.S., Bureau of the Census)*
- 71 % of all high school dropouts come from fatherless homes *(Source: National Principals Association Report on the State of High Schools)*
- 75 % of all adolescent patients in chemical abuse centers come from fatherless homes *(Source: Rainbows for all God's Children)*
- 63 % of youth suicides are from fatherless homes *(Source: U.S. D.H.H.S., Bureau of the Census)*

Juvenile Delinquency/Crime/Gangs

- 80 % of rapists motivated with displaced anger come from fatherless homes *(Source: Criminal Justice & Behavior, Vol 14, p. 403-26)*
- 70 % of juveniles in state-operated institutions come from fatherless homes *(Source: U.S. Dept. of Justice, Special Report)*
- 85 % of all youths sitting in prisons grew up in a fatherless home *(Source: Fulton Co. Georgia jail populations, Texas Dept. of Corrections)*

These statistics translate to mean that children from a fatherless home are:

- 5 times more likely to commit suicide
- 32 times more likely to run away
- 20 times more likely to have behavioral disorders
- 14 times more likely to commit rape

- 9 times more likely to drop out of high school
- 10 times more likely to abuse chemical substances
- 9 times more likely to end up in a state-operated institution
- 20 times more likely to end up in prison

Juveniles have become the driving force behind the nation's alarming increases in violent crime.

When a mother comes to Christ, her family will join her at church only 17% of the time; but when a father comes to Christ, his family joins him 93% of the time.

Over 70% of the boys who are being raised in church will abandon it during their teens and twenties. Many of these boys will never return.

A boy needs a guide, a dad, a mentor, a man who can explain to him those feelings he is having in his body, his mind, his heart. The fatherless boy longs for the dad who is not there. The abandonment physically or emotionally from the father runs deep into their being. It's crushing.

Initiation into boyhood, into manhood, is critical. Only a man can do this for a boy. He teaches him how to use his strength and power for good. He trains him to walk the ancient trail of the masculine heart. What the feelings for the girl or woman mean and how to treat her feelings in an honorable and healthy way.

One Saturday during our KOZ, we set up a challenge course. It had jumps and ropes and mud holes. The obstacles were relatively simple, but it didn't matter, the boys loved it. One obstacle was a rope swinging over a water tank. It was a short swing and just a few feet off the ground. About halfway through the day one of the little guys swung out and slipped as he crossed the water tank. He tumbled to the ground and almost immediately started crying. When it became apparent he needed attention, we moved in. After a few minutes we decided to take him to the fire station around the corner to get him checked by our EMS friends. He went from there to the hospital; his arm was broken. Later that day we went to visit him in the hospital and we began to apologize profusely to the parents. The mom stopped us in midsentence, "Hey, it's okay. He is a boy. We get it. It happens." For me, those parents get an A + for knowing what a boy even is.

We as KOZ men are fighting for the hearts and souls of the boys in our care. Does it mean they need slap fights and headlocks? No. Is that part of what they may experience along the trail? Yes. It is what they do with those things that they have to learn to navigate. Do you punch a bully? Can you play outside in 100-degree temperature? Can you fix a flat tire? Can you start a camp fire, shoot a gun or bow, catch a fish? Yes, yes, they need to understand the way of a man. To do that, they may have to get a few stiches, a little road rash. They will need a man to show them how to fix a broken water pipe. But they are designed for that—it is our being. A boy who does not have those lessons can wander his whole life looking for who he is. His heart deeply wounded.

PROVERBS 22:29, "Do you see a man skillful in his work? He will stand before kings; he will not stand before obscure men."

1 CORINTHIANS 16:13–14, "Be watchful, stand firm in the faith, act like men, be strong. Let all that you do be done in love."

Yes, a boy can be validated, initiated, and trained to walk the uneven ground of life today as a good man. It takes a good man, a man of faith, a man who cares about him to make that happen. That is the mission the men of KOZ are on.

Every boy, in his journey to become a man,
takes an arrow in the center of his heart,
in the place of his strength. Because the wound
is rarely discussed and even more rarely healed,
every man carries a wound. And the wound
is nearly always given by his father.

JOHN ELDREDGE

"...KIDS WHO PLAY OUTSIDE ARE SMARTER,
HAPPIER, MORE ATTENTIVE,
AND LESS ANXIOUS THAN KIDS
WHO SPEND MORE TIME INDOORS."

CHAPTER 4

THE OUTDOORS

Boys are not going outdoors. Kids are staying inside. The average kid spends less than 40 minutes a week outside, 70 hours a week in front of a screen. Sit in that thought for a few minutes. That is a train wreck.

OUTDOOR HEALTH

So many adults when they hear those statistics reply, "When I was a kid all we did was play outside." "We never wanted to be inside." "We were told to stay outside and when the street lights came on, we knew it was time to head home." The temperature did not matter. We didn't care if we were hungry. We just wanted to play. We stared at the clouds passing over, laid in the fields in the dirt and grass. We climbed trees, jumped and rode our bikes, and swam in the creek. We drank from the garden hose and ate hotdogs, peanut butter, and potted meat from a can. We dreamed and created story lines in our minds. We explored the bugs and the nooks and crannies in the dirt, on the hill, along the fence. And we survived.

The Child Mind Institute published a letter on the effects of the outdoors and our kids. Their studies showed statistical and scientific findings that can't be denied.

"Recent studies have exposed the benefit—even necessity—of spending time outdoors, both for kids and adults. Some argue that it can be any outdoor environment. Some claim it has to be a "green" environment—one with trees and leaves. Others still have shown that just a picture of greenery can benefit mental health. These nuances aside, most of the studies agree that kids who play outside are smarter, happier, more attentive, and less anxious than kids who spend more time indoors."

The study lists the benefits. It builds confidence. It promotes creativity and imagination. It teaches responsibility. It provides different stimulation. It gets kids moving. It makes them think. It reduces stress and fatigue. According to the Attention Restoration Theory, urban environments require what's called directed attention, which forces us to ignore distractions and exhausts our brains. In natural environments, we practice an effortless type of attention known as soft fascination that creates feelings of pleasure, not fatigue.

OUTDOOR LEGACY

Hunting and fishing were once traditions passed down by the father, the uncle, the grandfather. Yes, in some families this continues. It is a beautiful thing. But the facts are, culturally, that is not happening. This generation is not only not going outside, but when they do, they are not even considering hunting or fishing.

A recent U.S. Fish and Wildlife Service five-year study of wildlife participation trends revealed that one participant group had a drastic decline. That would be the number of hunters.

Hunting participation declined by 2 million participants from 2011 to 2016 to 11.5 million. Total hunting expenditures declined 29 percent from $36.3 billion to $25.6 billion. This is a big deal. The industry announced in 2018 that if the trend is not reversed within ten years the hunters will lose their voice in policy and participation laws and rules. In short, the anti-hunting groups will be able to dictate where, when, what, and how we hunt, if at all.

FBOs (Faith Based Organizations) are rescuing our hunting heritage. They are fueling an R3 army: Rescue, Restore, and Rewild. They are hunters and mentors who are stepping in and training the next generation and re-fueling the older ones who once laid down their hunting rifles, bows, and fishing poles. Churches and other Christian organizations are building amazing mentoring programs across America and spending regular, quality time with kids, men, and families. KOZ is one of them.

"Few organizations know how to stir the hearts, souls, and spirits of budding outdoor enthusiasts like our partners at Kids Outdoor Zone. KOZ and their dedicated cadre of volunteers change the lives of kids forever through their unique offering of irreplaceable outdoor experiences, coupled with quality mentorship and ministry. The future of our proud outdoor and sporting heritage is in good hands thanks to KOZ." Carter Smith, Executive Director, Texas Parks and Wildlife

JESUS OUTDOORS

The book of John has the best scenario of how important the outdoors was to Jesus and why we should use His model. In chapter 21, Jesus is on the shore at sunrise. His best friends have been out fishing all night, unsuccessfully I might add. As they are coming in, He yells out, "How was your fishing?" A terrible question to a fisherman who has been out all night and got skunked. Jesus knew that. Then He told them to drop their nets, and when they did, they filled up with the biggest catch ever. They drug the nets in and Jesus asked them, "Bring some of that fresh fish over to my campfire." It was sunrise, lakeside, with a campfire, food, fellowship. It was one of the last times He would see His men and He wanted to be with them where they spent their most intimate moments, outside, around a campfire. This is where they were most nights the last three years with Him. Walking from town to town, camping at night. His men were training under the very stars He created. Jesus chose the outdoors over any other place to train His men. It is also the example He gave us where He went most often to be with His Father.

Why wouldn't we use this model? Why don't we train more of our men in the exact way Jesus did? Why would we not train our boys there, by a campfire on the edge of a lake? Fact of the matter is, we should.

*I'd rather be in the mountains
thinking of God than in church thinking
about the mountains.*

JOHN MUIR

CHAPTER 5

THE KOZ LEADER WIFE

I t seems far too often when a man is asked to do ministry, his wife is not included in the decision. Sure, he may come home and let her know that he is considering ministry work. He may ask her what she thinks. We have found that if a man is considering serious ministry like KOZ, he absolutely needs his wife to know what he is committing to and he needs her support.

When a man commits to KOZ he is committing to the boys he will mentor. He needs the time away from his family and work to be cleared of any distractions. Yes, he may bring his son and they participate together, but we found if his wife does not know the ministry and the level of commitment, she will not give it the weight it requires. She plans as usual outings, birthday parties, and family life on top of the KOZ calendar. We found when she understands the program and the need for him to be fully present, his success rate soars.

Becoming a KOZ leader includes a two-hour dinner that is all about the wives of the leaders who will train. A Friday night pot luck works great. During that time a video created just for the wives is played and talked about.

Topics in the video include the importance of her support. That she will again be asked to "cover the home front" for him while he is out on his Saturday morning KOZ events. It covers who her husband is going to mentor, the basic info on KOZ and the fatherless boys, their hurts and needs. The video also includes how she can be a key role in the success of the overall ministry. It invites her to utilize her gifts and skills as a follower and daughter of the King. She knows the single moms in the church and community. She can communicate the program of KOZ to them and how they can get their boys involved. It's truly a beautiful thing.

Sandra Greaney, TJ's wife, leads the communication and ministry efforts with the KOZ wives. That includes emails, prayer time, gifts, and more, exclusively for the wives of the KOZ men. Her gift of hospitality and joy bring a whole other level of inspiration to the ministry of KOZ.

As a wife you want your husband to lead your family. You want him to stand in the gap, be a warrior for the needy and fight for you and your family. Sadly, many men today have lost that edge or have never encountered the Holy Spirit in that capacity. Ladies, let me assure you one thing, if your husband does KOZ, if he truly steps into the ministry and goes deep into the mission of rescuing the boys, he will change. Not that he is bad or not a good man now, but he will change in ways you could only dream about. His walk with Jesus will go deeper, which means his love for you and his family will grow. He will step long into his walk, begin relationships with other strong men of God. Really, he will change.

Dear Wives of KOZ Men,

First, I want to say thank you. Thank you for supporting your husbands to reach out to the fatherless boys of our world. These boys are desperate for men to train them in healthy masculinity. They are the future young men who will ask our daughters to go out on dates, marry them, raise our grandchildren. What these KOZ men do matters so much to the future generation.

One summer day I was on a solo road trip to visit our daughter and began listening to a book on tape called *Wild at Heart* by John Eldredge. TJ had recently read the book and I could see something inside him changing. As I drove the back roads, the words spoken began to open my eyes to who he longed to be. I paused the recording several times to call TJ to say, "I understand now, I get it."

We, the wives of KOZ leaders, have a special bond. I want you to know that I am committed to our community and am here for you. We are sisters in Christ.

Much love and many thanks to you sisters. I consider it a true honor to share in the KOZ Wives Ministry with you. You are so loved and appreciated.

May peace and love be yours in abundance,
SANDRA GREANEY
Wife of TJ, KOZ Founder
Sandra@KidsOutdoorZone.com

"KOZ HAS BEEN A GROUP OF MEN THAT HAVE
DEMONSTRATED THE TRUE LOVE OF GOD.
THEY HAVE GIVEN HIM COMMITMENT, SUPPORT,
ENCOURAGEMENT—THE KIND THAT A BOY NEEDS
AND LONGS FOR FROM A MAN.

AS A SINGLE MOM, THEY HAVE FILLED AN AREA
IN MY SON'S HEART THAT I COULD NOT."

FOREVER GRATEFUL,
BEVERLY LUTICH

CHAPTER 6

THE MOM

Mama Bear. Letting Go is a Big Deal.

First and foremost, moms, single moms, we love you. We believe in you. We thank God for you. We know you have the toughest job in the world. We get it and we want to help.

There is a good chance that the single mom may struggle with letting her boy go on a KOZ outing. They don't want to drop them off and leave, they want to stay and watch. They don't want to let them stay overnight because they "aren't ready yet." They don't want to have them around guns because, pick a reason. They (moms) are designed to protect their young. A mama bear will absolutely shred anyone or anything that gets between her and her cubs. It is exactly how God made them. The love of a mother is essential in a boy growing up healthy. A mom's love, voice, and touch can sooth the heart, soul, and skinned knee.

Ah, but there is truth to moms becoming overly protective. A boy can be wounded deeply by an overly protective mom. That is fact.

Boys are hard wired to separate from a mom. This information is easily found documented in science and medical journals. They move from mothered to fathered. They seek to know from the dad, "Do I have what it takes?" They want to be challenged, explore, learn the ancient path to manhood. Falling from a tree, cutting their finger with a pocket knife, arguing with another boy then overcoming the confrontation. These are the things a man high fives a boy over and encourages him, trains him, to know he can survive. Many moms shudder at these confrontations and engagements of testosterone.

From Focus on the Family: *"There is no precise agreement among child-development experts as to how a boy grows into a healthy sense of his masculinity.*

"That said, we should add that while both parents are important, dads play a unique role in a boy's development. A male infant begins life in close contact with his mother. Later he makes the leap to identifying with his father. From there he moves on to participation in the larger "boyhood community" of his male peers. Each piece of the puzzle is important, and the entire process takes place over an extended period of time.

"Masculinity is much broader than one culture's expression of it; at its core, it's about initiating, self-sacrifice, speaking the truth, giving, protecting, defending, and reaching out to others.

"A boy needs to be affirmed as a male as he is, even if his form of expression doesn't fit his parents' pre-conceived notions of masculinity.

"Take steps to introduce him to the world of boys and men. This may require gentle strength and per-sistence—especially if a boy feels hurt and angry and has for this reason rejected his father. It also

means enlisting other healthy boys and men to be
part of your life and your son's life."

One of our mottos for KOZ is "Do Hard Things." It's super healthy. KOZ men will walk with boys and teach them to confront the hard things they will face at home, in school, in life. I rarely hear a good reason why a boy should not stay at a KOZ event and push through hard tasks and undertakings. A mom in many situations might say, "Just let him stop, that was good, we don't have to go all the way." She means well but it is not the way of the masculine journey. His heart, his soul, his mind grows when he is pushed past what he thinks is his limit in so many areas. In almost every case I have ever experienced, it was better for them to participate, face their fears, stay and fight to get through something, "Do Hard Things."

KOZ is designed for boys 8 to 18. Those are the formative years when a boy is breaking away. It was designed that way. The boys go from half a Saturday a month to maybe an overnight campout. Then maybe a hunting or fishing trip, a backpacking trip. They learn to trust men who will train them in life lessons, outdoor skills, and how to navigate as a young man.

Moms of KOZ boys who have been through this will tell you it mattered. It made a difference. Their boys grew taller that day, that weekend, that week away from them. They became more self-confident; they learned to walk a bit more sure-footed.

"It has been really great for Daniel, and I personal-
ly believe that training boys in Godly masculinity

is greatly lacking in so much of day to day life for boys—and even at church as boys are often asked to sit quietly or stand still and sing soft music. I love the part of the KOZ where they talk about being "dangerous for good," and the part of the pledge stating to "fight trouble together" with KOZ brothers, and the prayer that mentions being "strong and fierce warriors for [God]." I think that sometimes well-intentioned moms see this type of attitude as being too "aggressive" and even "ungodly," but I couldn't disagree more!! Boys need a place to be active in these ways and learn to fulfill these things in a Godly way and I'm thankful that KOZ supports this. Thank you for giving your time and energy and resources to KOZ - it is very impactful and is much appreciated!"
– Erika (A KOZ Mom)

I just wanted to extend a huge thank you. My son had a great time and it's something he could never experience if he was not a part of the group. These experiences have impacted him so much. He feels a sense of belonging which is a huge thing for kids his age. You are all making a difference and as a mom I am grateful. My son has conquered so many fears through this group. He would never try things and never want to. It's just amazing what outdoors and mentors do for a child's life. So thank you to all the group of guys that give up time and energy to pour into my son's life.
– Patty (A KOZ Mom)

We understand that the Mama Bear loves her boy, she doesn't want him hurt, and she is there (at KOZ) because she is feeling inside something is needed in his life. It is the job as the man, the trained KOZ leader, to explain to her the benefits of her trusting the KOZ men—to assure her that her son will be in good hands and it is a good thing for him to begin to ride his own trail. KOZ leaders understand the true dynamics of the mother/son relationship. They honor it. But they also challenge Mom to release her son into a world of men who will care for him, train him, be there for him. It is the way of the healthy male. It's the way of KOZ. KOZ Strong.

Raising boys has made me a more generous woman than I really am. Undoubtedly, there are other routes to learning the wishes and dreams of the presumably opposite sex, but I know of none more direct, or more highly motivating, than being the mother of sons.

MARY KAY BLAKELY

WOULDN'T IT BE COMPELLING IF WHAT WE DID
HELPED MEN PURSUE A LIFE WITH CHRIST
THAT INCLUDED SPIRITUAL GROWTH,
AS WELL AS BEING ON MISSION
WITH THE GREAT COMMISSION?

CHAPTER 7

THE CHURCH

To The Pastor

Pastor, what can be said that hasn't already been said about men, men's ministry, biblical masculinity, and male leadership that is so desperately needed in the church and society today. Faithful pastors, authors, speakers, and denominational leaders around the world and for generations now have beckoned repeatedly for men to step up, engage, and lead their families and their communities and churches.

As we travel the country and get to know pastors and their churches, men's ministry appears to have been placed on the back burner of many of our churches today. In some ways, I get it. Ministry to men can be hard ground. Men seem hesitant to be drawn into the latest Bible study or message to "be better." I'm sure there are a multitude of reasons for this—uncertainty and confusion about gender roles, shame from addictions such as pornography, distractions that come from the latest obsession—work or play, and unexplained anger from these or some other deeper wound. The enemy has an arsenal that he can use to keep a man off the front line of the battle for the lost in his community. And need I remind us that we are in a battle with a world at war? Our adversary will always fight to keep "a good man down."

Another reason for this male hesitancy may be that men are "doers." It's no coincidence that many men's ministry leaders (where it exists) are also the overseer of disaster relief in their church, state, or territory. For some churches, the only men's ministry is their firewood or widow's ministry. It's amazing how men will show up when a chainsaw, a pair of gloves, and a pick-up truck is needed! However, many of these same men won't darken the door of a small group or Bible study that requires reading and study and calls them to walk closer to their heavenly Father. While men remain in a state of hesitation and even being closed off, the vacuum of leadership they are leaving is catastrophic.

Pastor, do you have enough equipped, faithful, and ministry-ready men in your church right now to help lead, teach, and serve your church? What about enough men to lead, teach, and serve anywhere from 10 to 100 new families? My friend Mike Young, director of Nobel Warriors, challenges pastors with this very question. He also follows this question with, "What are you as pastor doing about that...could it be that growth in your church is hindered because we aren't intentional about growing men?" Equipping men for this battle has never been more important than it is today. Would you consider an alternative to traditional men's ministry that begins with serving? Would you consider tapping into a man's core needs that opens him up to be the "rescuer" before and while he is being transformed?

The deep and desperate needs of a man are to be trusted, empowered, and commissioned to a task, a great work, and a mighty adventure. Pastor, you can play a key role in unlocking the culture-changing authority and power God has given a man. Our normal mode of operandi can be "clean 'em up before you ask or encourage them to serve." This often plays out by calling men to Bible study and small groups, which are necessary and can be transformational. Usually, these are the only venues of growth and service offered men in a traditional church environment. We attend and speak at a lot of men's conferences. Often, the only tools offered men are volumes of awesome books and Bible studies. My question is, "Are these studies making a difference?" Do you ever wonder why men go to conferences or read these books (or not) and they become "better" men but are still hesitant to serve? Wouldn't it be compelling if what we did helped men pursue a life with Christ that included spiritual growth, as well as being on mission with the Great Commission?

Kids Outdoor Zone (KOZ) has experienced an awakening in men that, quite frankly, has surprised us. We have met many men, physically and metaphorically sitting on the back row of churches, struggling to see where they fit in the programming of the church. He may not teach or sing, and he has resigned himself to stacking chairs and taking up the offering. In the midst of his "service," he often finds himself wondering, "Is this all there is to living out the Christian faith?"

Recently I met David while he was attending a local men's conference with other men from his church. David came up to my KOZ booth and was struck by the offering of KOZ. KOZ is an outdoor ministry with an overarching goal of rescuing boys that are ages 8 to 18. Requiring a commitment of only one Saturday each month, KOZ provides these men an opportunity to make a significant difference in the lives of boys through intentional discipleship and mentorship.

Outdoor stuff, adventure, skills, and time with boys—David immediately knew he could do that. Not only could he do it, he had to do it! He went home and asked his pastor if he could begin a KOZ in their church. A guy seeking out engagement in a ministry that would meet a huge need in the church and community by providing an example of biblical masculinity to boys prompted the pastor to immediately say "yes!" Within a year, David's KOZ group has grown to over 15 boys, two of which he baptized in a local lake on their KOZ Saturday morning when they accepted Christ. There are far more stories than we can tell in this one chapter. However, they are coming in month after month as KOZ grows around the country. Suffice it to say, we have found a beautiful story of awakening, discipleship, and battle in the story of KOZ.

Pastor, I'd encourage you to make the adventure of KOZ available to your men. If your men are asking, please consider allowing them to step up to the call and embark on this journey with them. Though they may not be "cleaned up" and polished, rest assured that the Holy Spirit does that along the trail of their caring for boys that so desperately need a man in their lives. These boys need to unplug from the digital toxicity and step into creation with a Godly mentor to show them the way.

These boys are in the core mission of your church, your heart. They will be the next generation of men that will either be rescued and leading in the church as adults...or not. We can make a difference. Pastor, you can make a difference!

Anything you can do that connects believers with one another engages the church to go to the next level, which keeps the pastor from being burnt out, which therefore keeps him in the ministry.

TONY EVANS

STRUCTURE, DIRECTION, LOVE, ADVENTURE,
AND BIBLICAL PRINCIPLES ARE THE KEY TO A BOY FEELING
A PART OF SOMETHING IMPORTANT AND
LEARNING TO TRUST THE MEN WHO LEAD HIM.

CHAPTER 8

THE SATURDAY MORNING

The topics and curriculum for a KOZ Saturday morning are provided in advance each month. Studies have shown boys do better when they have discipline and structure. Here is an example of some of the material and how it might read or look during a KOZ Saturday.

KOZ Monthly Outdoor Training[©]
JUNE CAMPING ADVENTURE

7:30 LEADER MEETING
AND PRAYER TIME

This time is imperative and gives you time to prepare your hearts for the meeting and time with the boys. Do not take this time lightly. Be on time, meet with God first.

Boys begin to arrive and the meeting begins. All together say the American Pledge of Allegiance (or your country pledge) then the KOZ Prayer:

Lord, thank you for making us strong and fierce warriors for you. We hunt, we fish, and we share our faith with others. God Bless America (your country). Amen

THE LEADER'S FIRST QUESTIONS, DISCUSSION ON THE OUTDOOR ADVENTURE FOR THE DAY.

"Camping can be one of the easiest and best ways you can spend time outdoors doing cool stuff with the boys. Sitting by a campfire, smores, laughing, telling stories, looking at the stars."

"Camping comes in all sorts of ways. Minimal gear, backpacking, car camping, and everything in-between. The one common thread—it is all super fun if you are prepared."

The KOZ leaders move into the beginning of the heart (Biblical) training immediately after talking about the outdoor topic.

SCRIPTURE TRAINING:
Leader's first questions, discussion.
This Month's Scripture:

1 CORINTHIANS 4:15, "For though you have countless guides in Christ, you do not have many fathers. For I became your father in Christ Jesus through the gospel."

The leaders begin conversation. June is the month of Father's Day. Have you ever had an older man, "a guide," teach you anything? What did they show you, what did you learn? Some of us have great dads that show us and teach us; they are "guides" in this life. But many of us don't have that dad or other man showing us outdoor skills and how to do life. That's what these men are doing here at KOZ. There are other "countless" guides around the country working with boys just like you guys—showing you the way. Over the course of a boy's life, you will see many different men showing you many different things. This verse says that God has many guides in Christ. Be sure and thank God for these men. As you get older and learn more and more, you are becoming guides for others as you continue to learn also.

If you have a dad that is involved in your life, be sure to remember to honor him on Father's Day.

OUTDOOR TRAINING

As soon as the heart conversation is over for the morning, the KOZ leaders begin the outdoor training.

Camping is a lifelong lesson you can teach the boys. This month should include the solid basics and some amazing extras. Tents. Bring all kinds. Have the boys put them up, take them down, fit them in their holding bags. Have a race on who can put one up correctly first, take it down, and pack it away. Sleeping bags. The new sleeping quilts. How are they rated for cold, comfort, and materials? Lots to learn here. Where to set up a camp: Look for flat area. Not under dead branches. Not near flash flood areas.

There is so much to do here. Set up stations and rotate the boys. Go visit a local, state, or national park to show them places they can camp after you have taught them. Have the park ranger talk with them about camping at the park.

Each month includes two Trail Maps: These give the KOZ leaders (HTLs—Harvest Team Leaders) examples of how to have a conversation with the boys.

Trail Map #1:

If you had to go have brain surgery and you could pick your doctor, would you chose your buddy sitting next to you right there in KOZ or would you want a doctor who went to school, learned everything, and has done lots of brain surgery? I would pick the doctor. Why? Because he has learned from people who did it before him. They taught him how to do it. He could trust his teachers and if he did what they taught him, he would do well on your brain. Maybe even learn things to teach others.

Every guy needs men in his life. Young guys, older guys, every guy. KOZ can be a safe place for you. If you don't have a dad, KOZ leaders want you to know they care about you. They are sad your dad is not there, but they are here and they will be here for you. God made KOZ so you would not have to be alone on this trail. Trust your KOZ leaders, ask them the questions you need answers for.

Trail Map #2:

Camping is a great activity to do with someone who knows what they are doing – right?! If you've never built a fire, cooked on a fire, or set up a tent, it's really good to have someone who has done that before. Guides are important and God has made them "countless" for us. We need guides to show us how to camp, how to walk with Jesus, how to be respectful to others, how to learn to drive, how to — the list could go on and on. If we don't have a guide, we tend to struggle more and make more mistakes. That makes life harder, and it is harder to understand. Identify someone in your life, maybe one of the KOZ leaders, that you trust as a guide for you and talk to him about something you would like to know more about and would enjoy being shown how to do.

Also, be sure to honor your dad on Father's Day. Think and pray about how to do that better than ever before. Dads are special and deserve your honor and respect.

WRAPPING UP THE DAY

Near the end of the day and before lunch, the boys go to the **KOZ Sit Spot**. A quiet place outdoors where they can think about the day. The leaders will pass out a blank index card and pen. The boys are instructed to write one thing they learned and anything the leaders can be praying for this upcoming month until they meet again.

After lunch and before the parents come, the boys work to earn their KOZ Dog Tags. These are levels of achievement in Bible study and other tasks.

Of course, there are more materials and details to each meeting. They may seem simple, but they are profound in the boys' lives. Structure, direction, love, adventure, and biblical principles are the key to a boy feeling a part of something important and learning to trust the men who lead them.

"I SOLEMNLY PLEDGE UNDER OATH THAT I WILL
NEVER LEAVE MY KOZ BROTHERS BEHIND.
I WILL ALWAYS BE KIND TO THEM, HELP THEM
WHEN THEY LOOK LIKE THEY HAVE TOO MUCH,
RUN TO THEM WHEN THEY YELL FOR HELP, GIVE THEM
THE BEST SEAT AND FIRST CHANCE AT EVERYTHING.
THEY ARE MY BROTHERS; WE FIGHT TROUBLE TOGETHER."

CHAPTER 9
TO A NEW KOZ BOY

I don't know if many of you guys (KOZ boys) will read this, you young guys, but we did not want to leave you out if there are some who are thinking about KOZ or your mom is asking you to come to a meeting.

One of the best gifts you could ever have or want is not one you can order from Amazon. Walmart does not have it. It's not a video game, a motorcycle, or a tank. One of the best things about it, too, is that it is free. You will never have to pay for it ever, as long as it is the real thing. You know what it is, you have always wanted it even if you never said it out loud.

Every guy, no matter how old or how young, we all want and need a good friend.

There was a high school coach one time who called the KOZ office and said, "Okay, I have got to know what this KOZ program is. He said, "I have the most popular boy in school and one of the quietest and unknown boys becoming great friends. When I asked how they met and why they are hanging out, they said they were both KOZ guys, friends."

That is what KOZ is. It's guys getting together, outside, and learning about some really, really crazy cool stuff. What guy doesn't like to go fishing? All of us guys need to know some kind of survival skills and what to do if the zombie apocalypse happens. When you do stuff like that with other guys, you get to know each other, rely on each other, and you become friends. Sometimes, really good friends. Most guys who come to KOZ have never met before, and once you come, you are a part of KOZ. That is the rule.

Each of you has a skill or something you are good at, maybe really good at, and those things might help another guy in KOZ. There may be some tools you had no idea about, and when you learn about them you find out you like it and are really good at using it. The army is made up of a bunch of guys who are really good at different things. Alone they are good, together they are great. You add to KOZ, you matter, and you will make your KOZ group better.

If you are in KOZ, there is an honor code you will learn. An honor code is something a man agrees to and it tells a person who you are, how you will act, what they can expect from you.

"I solemnly pledge under oath that I will never leave my KOZ brothers behind. I will always be kind to them, help them when they look like they have too much, run to them when they yell for help, give them the best seat and first chance at everything. They are my brothers; we fight trouble together."

The leaders in KOZ are special. These are men who care about you. You might say, "How can they care about me if I have never met them?" Good question. They want to be there. You don't have to worry if they are going to show up, if they are going to be there, because they will. It's an honor code, it's a commitment they made, and they won't break it. That is something special in a man, and your KOZ leaders are those kind of men.

When Mr. Rick and I were growing up, we didn't have a dad around. Some guys do, some guys don't. Maybe you do, maybe you don't. We didn't. The cool thing is, we had a few men in our lives who did exactly what your KOZ leaders are going to do for you. Teach you things all guys need to know. Listen to you when you have a question or need to talk. They care about you. Every young guy needs an older guy he can trust and count on. Your KOZ leaders will be that man for you.

KOZ is not a Sunday school class. You won't have to answer Bible questions and be bored listening to a bunch of stuff that you don't know about. The talks we have about our lives and Jesus are around a pond, around a fire pit, in a deer stand, or while hiking along a trail. We do want you to know about Jesus. He is really the whole reason KOZ works. All of your leaders have learned about Him and have seen Him work in their lives in some amazing ways and they want you to know just how amazing He can be in your life. No, you don't have to be a guy who goes to church. You might want to at some point, but it is not required to be a part of KOZ. What your KOZ leader wants you to know is that God is real, He is important, and He cares. You will see that by the way your leaders care about you.

If no one has told you lately, you need to know, you matter. You are awesome. God has a plan for you, and sometimes when things are hard and don't make a lot of sense, it might be hard to believe. You have a lot of gifts and a lot to offer other people. It always helps to know that and to hear it from other guys. We mean it and we want you to hear it from us.

Our challenge to you is to come to a KOZ meeting three times before you make a decision not to come back. It may not be your thing and you might not like it—fair enough because you tried. Your mom will be proud of you for trying, and who knows, you might just like it. We think you will.

God Bless,

Mr. TJ and Mr. Rick

It's not who I am underneath,
but what I do that defines me.

BATMAN

THE CLOSE

There was a terrible explosion at a fertilizer plant in Texas on April 17, 2013. A little boy that lived nearby bore a broken heart with the loss of his uncle in the explosion. He thought it was his fault his uncle ran to the scene of the fire and explosion. His mom found out about KOZ and soon after got him involved. During that time in KOZ, he began to understand it was not his fault and his heart began to heal. Several months later, his grandfather told us something amazing, "I just want to tell you thank you for giving me my grandson back. He was so wounded. The time at KOZ is so good for him. Thank you."

The wife of a KOZ leader wrote us recently, one of many who have. "Thank you for KOZ. My husband is a leader in KOZ and it has made him a different man, father, believer. I prayed for years for him to lead us, to find his place in church, with Jesus. Today because of what his heart has learned at KOZ, he does."

We hear these stories often about the boys, single moms, KOZ men being changed. Families, lives changed. Many for eternity by asking Jesus into their hearts or recommitting to their walk with Jesus. We see boys being baptized by their leaders in creeks, lakes, rivers, and horse troughs. We see the men of KOZ rise up in their walk. It is a beautiful thing. But it's not about KOZ.

Kids Outdoor Zone is a ministry, yes, but it is not KOZ that saves a life—it is Jesus. We give Him full credit for what KOZ is, what it does, and how it affects the boys, the men, the families.

We truly believe that the model of KOZ is one way Jesus used, a lot, to reach his men. The men drawn to KOZ are the men just like the ones He chose.

The mission field is all around us and there is much to do. Look next door, visit any school, walk down any city street and you will see it. Boys everywhere, and half are lost and hurting, the other half would love to be a part of an outdoor adventure.

The men of the church are the army Jesus was building. He calls them to stand in the gap, rescue the needy, and train up the boys. So the question is, why don't we? Why wouldn't we spend one Saturday morning a month changing the eternal destination of the next generation of men? We should. So, men, "Mount Up."

THE MISSION FIELD IS ALL AROUND US
AND THERE IS MUCH TO DO.

THE MEN OF THE CHURCH ARE THE ARMY
JESUS WAS BUILDING. HE CALLS THEM TO STAND IN THE GAP,
RESCUE THE NEEDY, AND TRAIN UP THE BOYS.
SO THE QUESTION IS, WHY DON'T WE?

MEN, "MOUNT UP."

ABOUT THE FOUNDER
OF KOZ

TJ GREANEY

TJ is an award-winning out-door travel and adventure writer, photographer, radio show host, and past President of the Texas Outdoor Writers Association. He published a Texas lifestyle magazine for more than 20 years with his wife, Sandra, from their home in Austin, Texas.

TJ and Sandra have three adult children. Cody Ryan, a professional bass angler, married to the amazing Nicole and parents of the most awesome granddaughter, Saylor. Taylor, an agriculture teacher in the Austin, Texas, area and married to CJ, parents of the brilliant Brady, grandson extraordinaire. Jon-Michael, the youngest, is an artist and mountain climber whose heart for adventure is waiting for the right gal.

If you ask TJ his passions, he would tell you: Jesus Christ, his family including dear friends, the ministry of KOZ, writing, coffee, the cool air of the mountains, and time on the ranch, any ranch.

Contact him at TJ@KidsOutdoorZone.com.

ABOUT THE COO AND
EAST COAST DIRECTOR OF KOZ

A native Mississippian, Rick is an outdoorsman at heart. He earned a Bachelor of Science in Forest Products from Mississippi State University in 1990 and a Master of Arts and Religion–Christian Leadership from Liberty University in 2019.

RICK MAGEE

After years of working in the paper and wood products industry, Rick surrendered to God's call to ministry in 2004 and served for fourteen years as the administrative and men's pastor at Hyland Heights Baptist Church in Rustburg, Virginia. He has served as the Chief of Operations for KOZ since 2016.

Married to his best friend Martha, they have three grown sons. Ethan, his oldest, served four years in the Marine Corp and now attends Liberty University. He and his wife, Rani, reside in Lynchburg, Virginia with their 2-year-old (angelic) daughter, Emery. Caleb resides in Rustburg, Virginia, and attends Liberty University. Josh lives in Roanoke, Virginia, and works as an A&P Mechanic for a local airline.

Rick loves Jesus, his family, a good bow stand in the fall, and a rod and reel in the spring. For Rick, there's nothing better than creating ministry opportunities using God's great outdoors!

Contact him at Rick@KidsOutdoorZone.com.

NOTES

Made in the USA
Middletown, DE
27 February 2023